HOW IT HAPPENS
at the Motorcycle Plant

By Shawndra Shofner
Photographs by Bob and Diane Wolfe

CLARA
HOUSE
BOOKS

Minneapolis

For my dear children: Benjamin, Brandon, and Breanna—SS
The publisher would like to thank the employees of Victory Motorcycles for their generous help with this book.
All photographs by Bob and Diane Wolfe except pp. 1, 3, 9, 31, and back cover (Victory Motorcycles).

Clara House Books
The Oliver Press, Inc.
Charlotte Square
5707 West 36th Street
Minneapolis, MN 55416-2510

Library of Congress Cataloging-in-Publication Data
Shofner, Shawndra.
   How it happens at the motorcycle plant / by Shawndra Shofner ;
photographs by Bob and Diane Wolfe.
        p. cm.
   Includes index.
   ISBN 1-881508-99-4
  1. Motorcycles–Design and construction–Juvenile literature. I.
Title. II. Title: At the motorcycle plant.
   TL440.15.S56 2006
   629.227'5–dc22

                                                                2006021832

ISBN 1-881508-99-4
Printed in the United States of America
10 09 08 07   8 7 6 5 4 3 2 1

Whether they're screaming around a race track, traveling in a rumbling pack, or parked alongside a country road, motorcycles signal outdoor fun. People ride motorcycles for entertainment, vacation travel, or to get to and from work. These sleek, comfortable vehicles are fuel efficient and safer than ever. Explore how one manufacturer creates motorcycles that thousands of people use every day for work and play.

Welding

The first step in building a motorcycle is creating its parts from steel, aluminum, and copper. Metal pieces are joined together by welding—heating and melting them at the spot where they meet. Steel melts at a scorching 700°F (371°C), so welders wear fire-proof vests, gloves, and masks to protect their eyes.

Some parts are made with the help of **robots**. Pieces of a motorcycle's frame—the structure that holds the engine, wheels, and handlebars—are attached to a welding rack. The rack flips over into the shelter and a robotic arm welds all the pieces together.

When the robot finishes welding, the rack flips back out of the shelter. A worker removes the hot frame from the rack with tongs and places it in a safe area to cool.

Paint

Color adds personality to the motorcycle. Parts, such as frames, fenders, and foot pegs, are painted in colors like flame yellow, supersonic blue, or stone beige. Here, unpainted gas tanks are mounted on a moving track that travels to a paint booth.

Paint comes from hoses attached to containers outside the paint booth. A computer tells the robotic arm what color to spray on the parts.

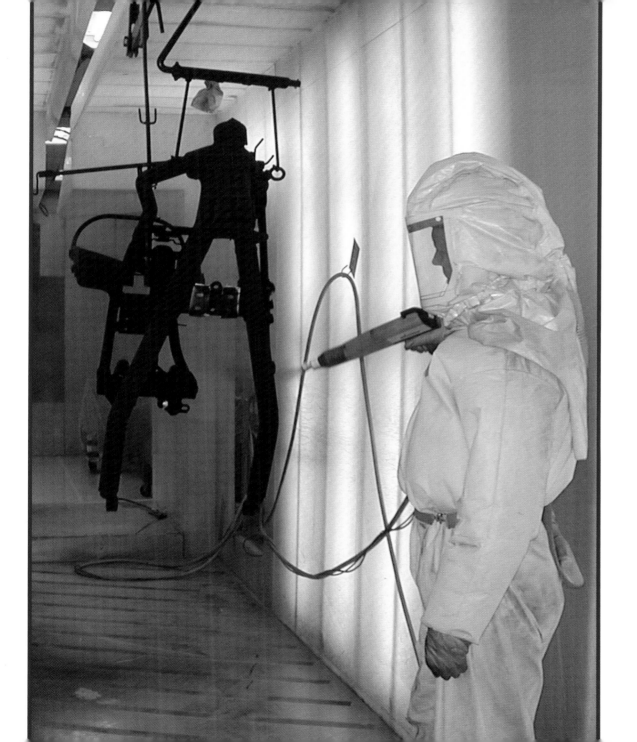

Not all painting is done by robots. This worker wears a protective suit and uses a spray gun to coat a part with powdered paint. The paint is electrically charged so it acts like a magnet and sticks to the metal. Unused powder paint is drawn through filters and used again.

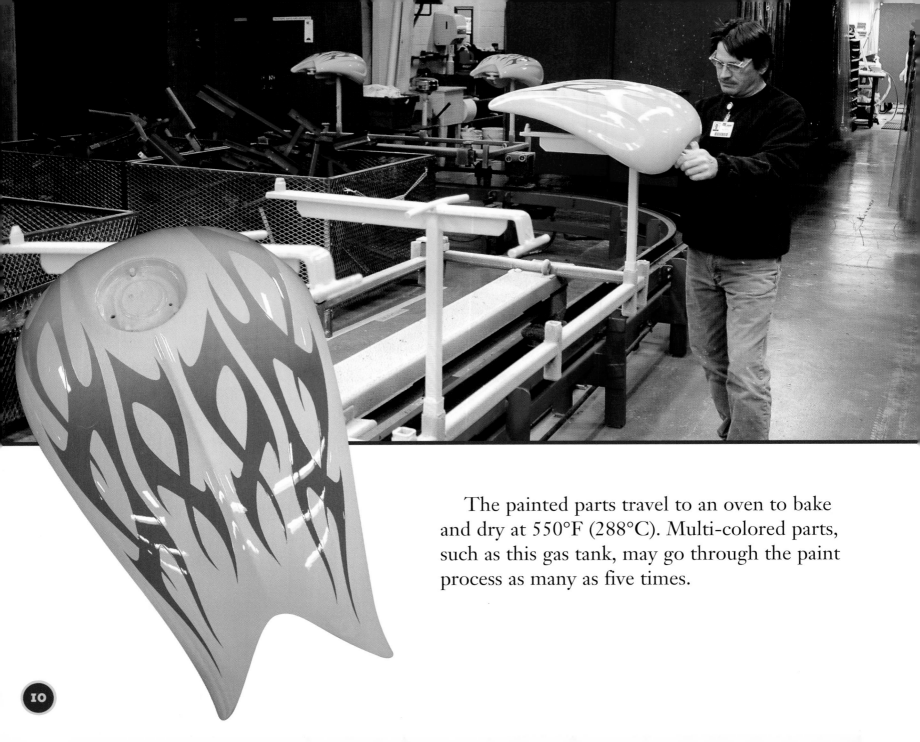

The painted parts travel to an oven to bake and dry at 550°F (288°C). Multi-colored parts, such as this gas tank, may go through the paint process as many as five times.

Finessing

Workers check every painted part for flaws, such as scratches or heat bubbles, and repair them. The workers buff the paint to a smooth shine with a spinning sponge dipped in soapy water. Here, a worker carefully polishes a fender by hand with a soft cloth. This process of making sure all parts are flawless is called **finessing**.

Workers store the parts on rubber-coated shelves or racks to keep them from being damaged. Now they are ready for the assembly line.

Assembly

A worker bolts the motorcycle **engine** to a hanging beam that travels from station to station where other workers add parts to it.

Each station contains the part or parts that will be installed, as well as tools, nuts, bolts, and other necessary materials. Colored bins help workers keep their parts organized.

A **hydraulic lift** helps this worker move the heavy frame to the engine. Each engine weighs about 300 pounds.

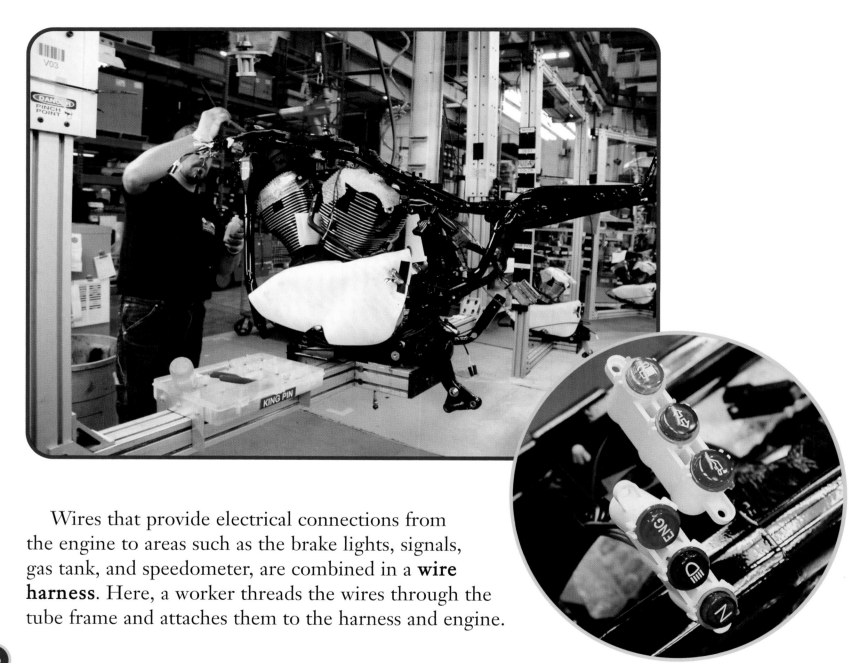

Wires that provide electrical connections from the engine to areas such as the brake lights, signals, gas tank, and speedometer, are combined in a **wire harness**. Here, a worker threads the wires through the tube frame and attaches them to the harness and engine.

Belts, wires, and small parts that can't easily be seen on the finished motorcycle are installed at some stations. Other stations add brake fluid and grease to keep the motorcycle running smoothly. This worker installs brake lines, the strong, flexible cables that control a motorcycle's ability to stop.

After the handlebars are secured, a worker hooks up a **hand control** box to the engine with wires that look like cables on a 10-speed bike. The left-hand control operates the clutch and turn signals. The right control powers the front brake and starter button.

The headlight and front signal lights are installed and connected to the wire harness.

Tires are fitted with rims and filled with air. Soapy water makes it easier for the rim to slip into the tire. Sometimes, a loud POP! sounds out as the air-filled tire seals against the rim.

This worker installs a rear tire with an automatic screwdriver.

This worker attaches the rear fender. Then, the rear lights are attached and plugged in, the license plate holder is bolted on, and the gas tank is mounted.

These
workers install
the exhaust
pipes and the
seat.

The last part added to the motorcycle is the engine cover.

Testing

A test driver rides a motorcycle on a treadmill to make sure everything works properly.

Packaging

A worker pushes the motorcycle onto a platform. An open-sided metal crate is built around the motorcycle that protects it when it is moved or shipped.

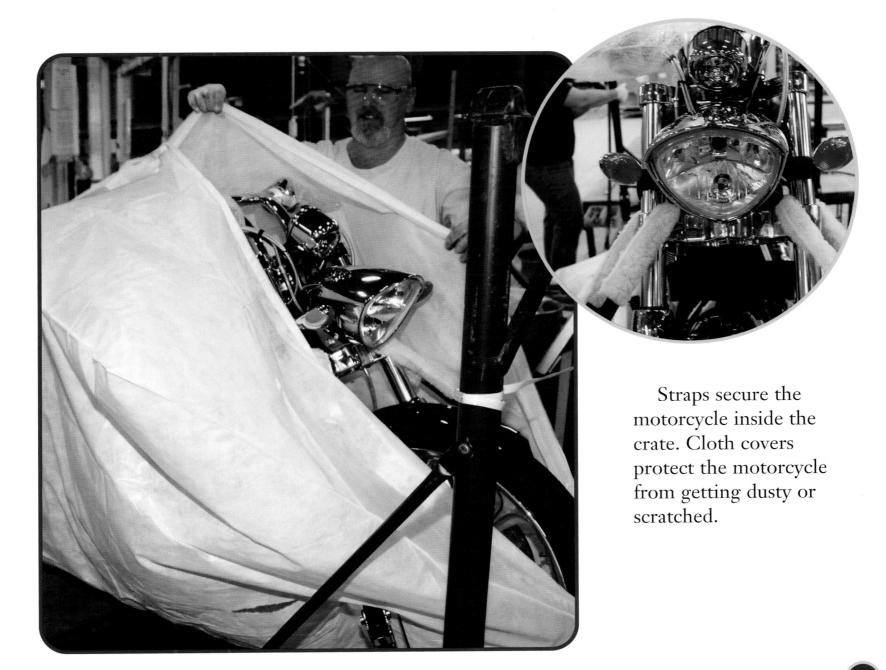

Straps secure the motorcycle inside the crate. Cloth covers protect the motorcycle from getting dusty or scratched.

A worker uses a forklift to move the heavy motorcycle crate to the last stage in packaging.

Workers cover the crate with a large plastic bag. A shrink-wrap machine heats the plastic until it fits snugly. The sealed crate is loaded onto a truck and sent to a **dealership**.

Dealerships display many motorcycle models in showrooms. Customers can test-drive their favorite model before they buy.

Whether they are driving for work or play, motorcyclists enjoy comfortable, safe, and fuel-efficient transportation. No wonder motorcycles are among the most popular vehicles throughout the world.

Glossary

dealership: a store where motorcycles are sold

engine: the part that powers the motorcycle

finessing: a process by which workers make sure the paint on parts is flawless

hand control: a part near the motorcycle's handles that drivers use to give the engine commands

hydraulic lift: a special tool used to move heavy objects

robots: programmed machines that perform tasks

wire harness: a set of wires that provides electrical connections from the engine to other parts

Index

Websites

Victory Motorcycles: www.victorymotorcycles.com
Motorcycle Safety Foundation: www.msf-usa.org
The Motorcycle Hall of Fame Museum: www.motorcyclemuseum.org